How Do I Love Thee?

Published in Australia by Australian Inspiration 2016

www.australianinspiration.com.au

Cover, design and typesetting by Luke Harris

www.workingtype.com.au

ISBN 978-0-9944731-5-8

How Do I Love Thee?

edited by

Chrissie Anthony

How do I love thee? Let me count the ways.

Elizabeth Barrett Browning
1806–1861, Sonnet 43

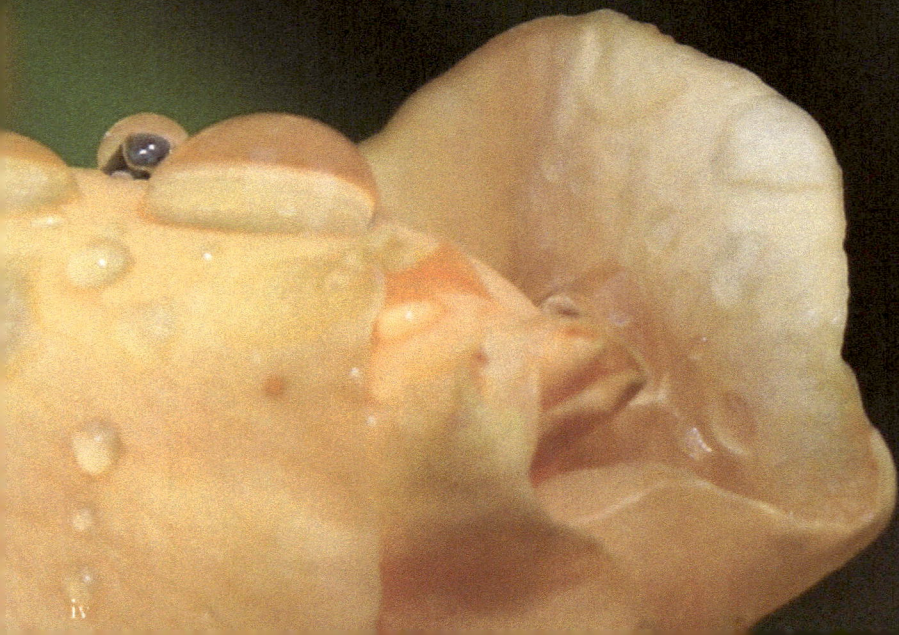

Introduction

How Do I Love Thee? Instinctively I respond, *Let me count the ways.* Whilst the author may slip from memory, if ever known, the wisdom of the ages live on. Enduring words of love, endearing sentiments that embrace us, that bind us. Love is universal. As is the need to express that love.

How Do I Love Thee? is a celebration of love. A lover's repertoire. Timeless love quotes married with images of another enduring love – the beauty and bounty of my garden. So you, too can say to your loved one,

How do I love thee?

Let me count the ways...

If I had a flower for every time I thought of you...

I could walk through my garden forever.

Alfred Lord Tennyson
1809–1892

Love looks not with the eyes, but with the mind;

And therefore is winged Cupid painted blind.

William Shakespeare
1564–1616, A Midsummer Night's Dream

A loving heart is the truest wisdom.

Charles Dickens
1812–1870

Where there is love there is life.

Mahatma Gandhi
1869–1948

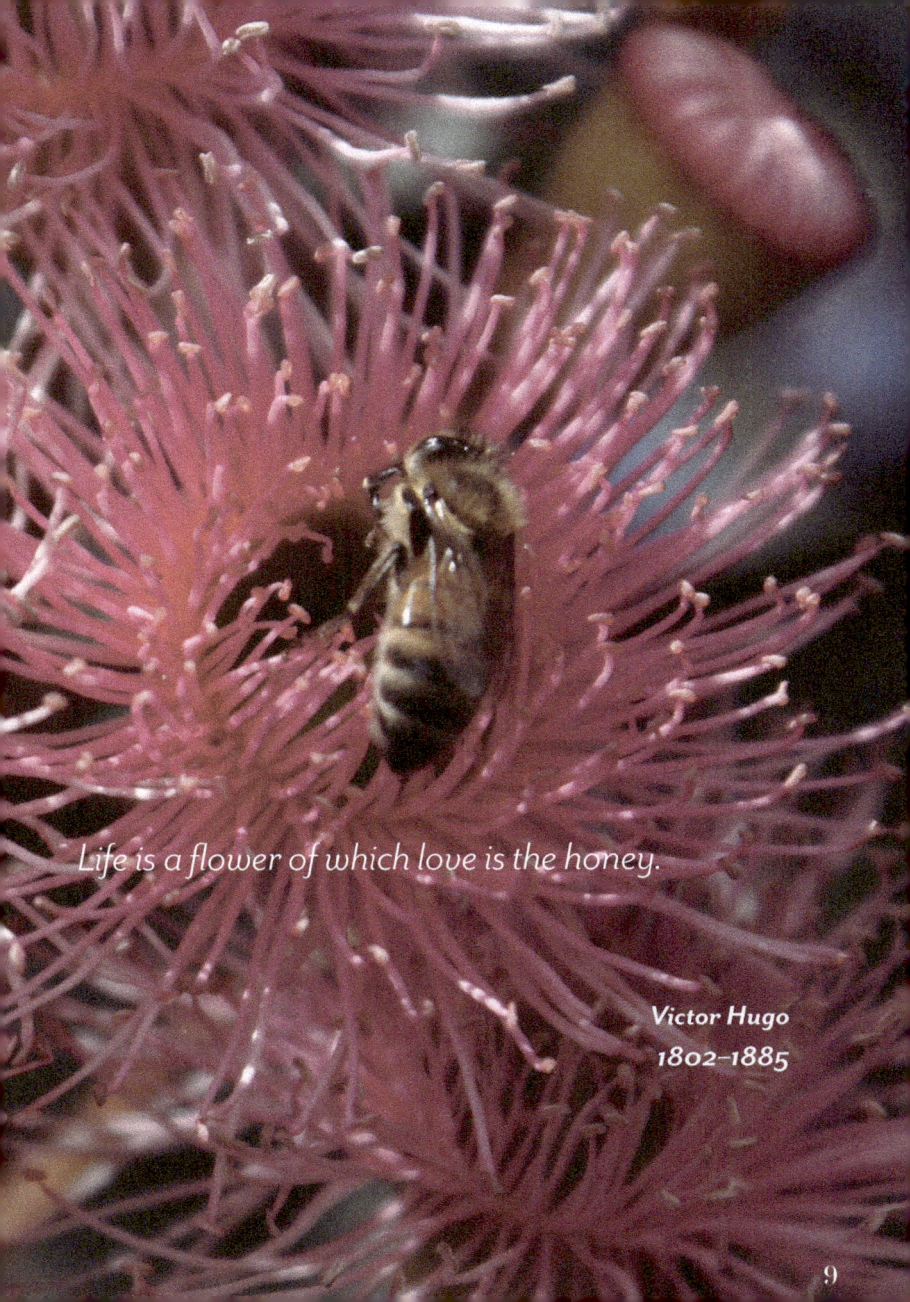

Life is a flower of which love is the honey.

Victor Hugo
1802–1885

Soul meets soul on lovers' lips.

Percy Bysshe Shelley
1792–1822, Prometheus Unbound

For small creatures such as we the

vastness is bearable only through love.

Carl Sagan
1934–1996

Love doesn't make the world go round.

Love is what makes the ride worthwhile.

Franklin P. Jones
1887–1929

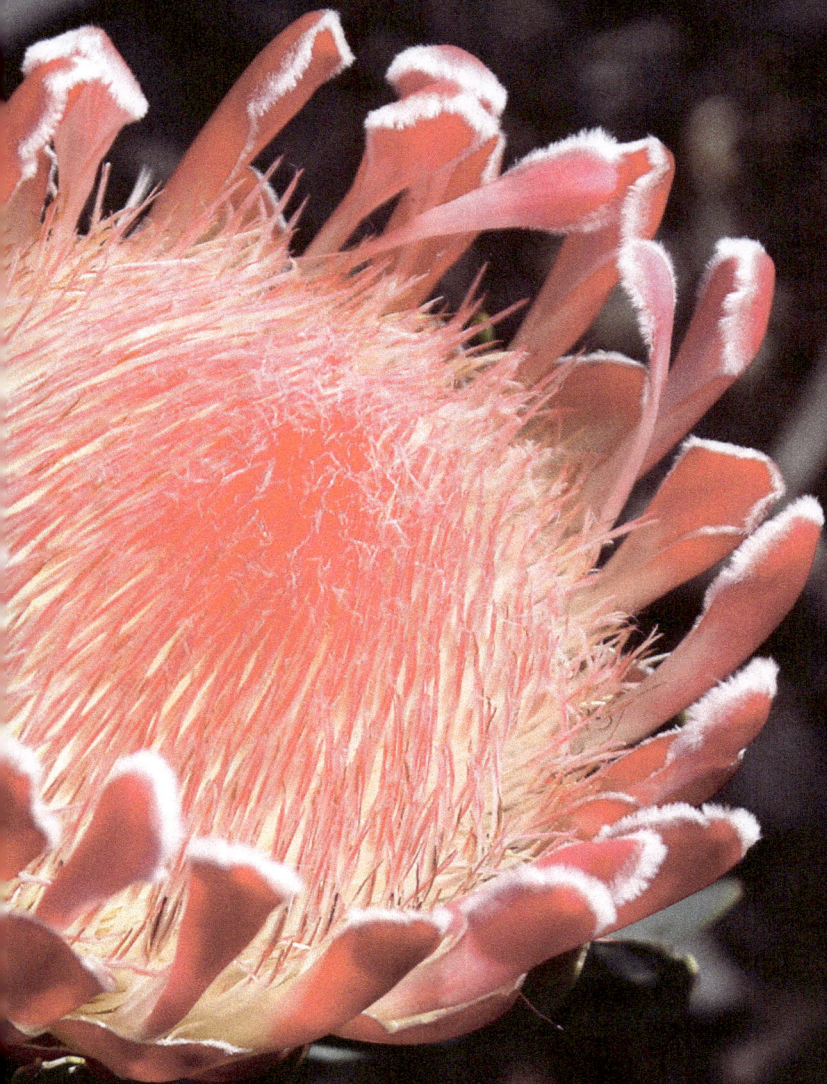

My love is like a red, red rose

That's newly sprung in June.

Robert Burns
1759–1796, A Red, Red Rose

Love loves to love love.

James Joyce
1882–1941

Love is the flower of life, and blossoms unexpectedly and without law, and must be plucked where it is found, and enjoyed for the brief hour of its duration.

D.H. Lawrence
1885–1930

The heart has its reasons that

reason does not know.

Blaise Pascal
1623–1662

Life without love is like a tree

without blossoms or fruit.

Khalil Gibran
1883–1931, The Prophet

The love we give away

is the only love we keep.

Elbert Hubbard
1856-1915

Age does not protect you from love. But love, to some extent, protects you from age.

Anaïs Nin
1903–1977

Love does not dominate;

it cultivates.

Johann Wolfgang Von Goethe
1749–1832

O love, what strange and wonderful fits:

one sole thing, one beauty alone, can

give me life and deprive me of wits.

Gaspara Stampa
1523–1554

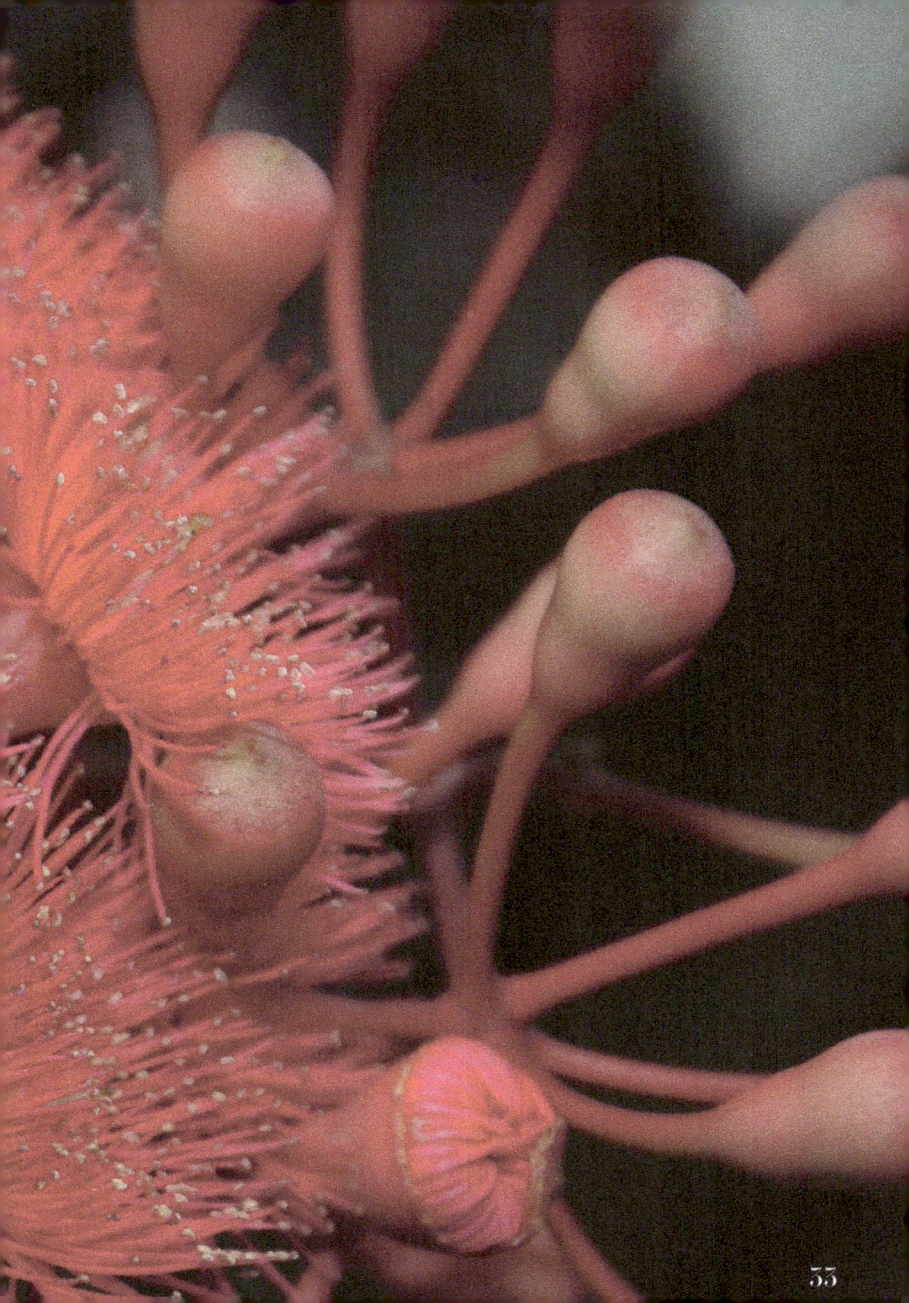

Love is of all passions the strongest,

for it attacks simultaneously the

head, the heart and the senses.

Lao Tzu
604 BC–531 BC

Love is our true destiny. We do not

find the meaning of life by ourselves

alone – we find it with another.

Thomas Merton
1915-1968

Love is a friendship set to music.

Joseph Campbell
1904–1987

You own my heart and mind;

I truly adore you.

Prince
1958–2016, Adore lyrics

Love is a promise; love is a souvenir,

Once given never forgotten, never let it disappear.

John Lennon
1940–1980, Advice For The Young At Heart *lyrics*

Yours is the light by which my

spirit's born: you are my sun,

my moon, and all my stars.

E.E. Cummings
1894–1962

If you wished to be loved, love.

Lucius Annaeus Seneca
4 BC–65 AD

Love is quivering happiness.

Khalil Gibran
1883-1931, Love Letters In The Sand

Love – bittersweet, irrepressible –

loosens my limbs and I tremble.

Sappho
circa 630–570 BCE

Love to faults is always blind;

Always is to joy inclin'd,

Lawless, wing'd, and unconfin'd,

And breaks all chains from every mind.

William Blake
1757–1827, Gnomic Verses

If I know what love is, it is because of you.

Herman Hesse
1877–1962

I like not only to be loved,

but also to be told I am loved.

George Eliot
1819–1880

A woman knows the face of

the man she loves as a sailor

knows the open sea.

Honore De Balzac
1799–1850

The best and most beautiful

things in this world cannot be

seen or even heard, but must be

felt with the heart.

Helen Keller
1880–1968

Love one another, but make not

a bond of love: Let it rather be a

moving sea between the shores

of your souls.

Khalil Gibran
1883–1931

Love is the emblem of eternity;

it confounds all notion of time;

effaces all memory of a beginning,

all fear of an end.

Germaine De Staël
1766–1817

'Tis better to have lost and loved

than never to have loved at all.

Alfred Lord Tennyson
1809–1892, In Memoriam

Time is nothing.

The desire to love is everything.

Nostradamus
1503–1556

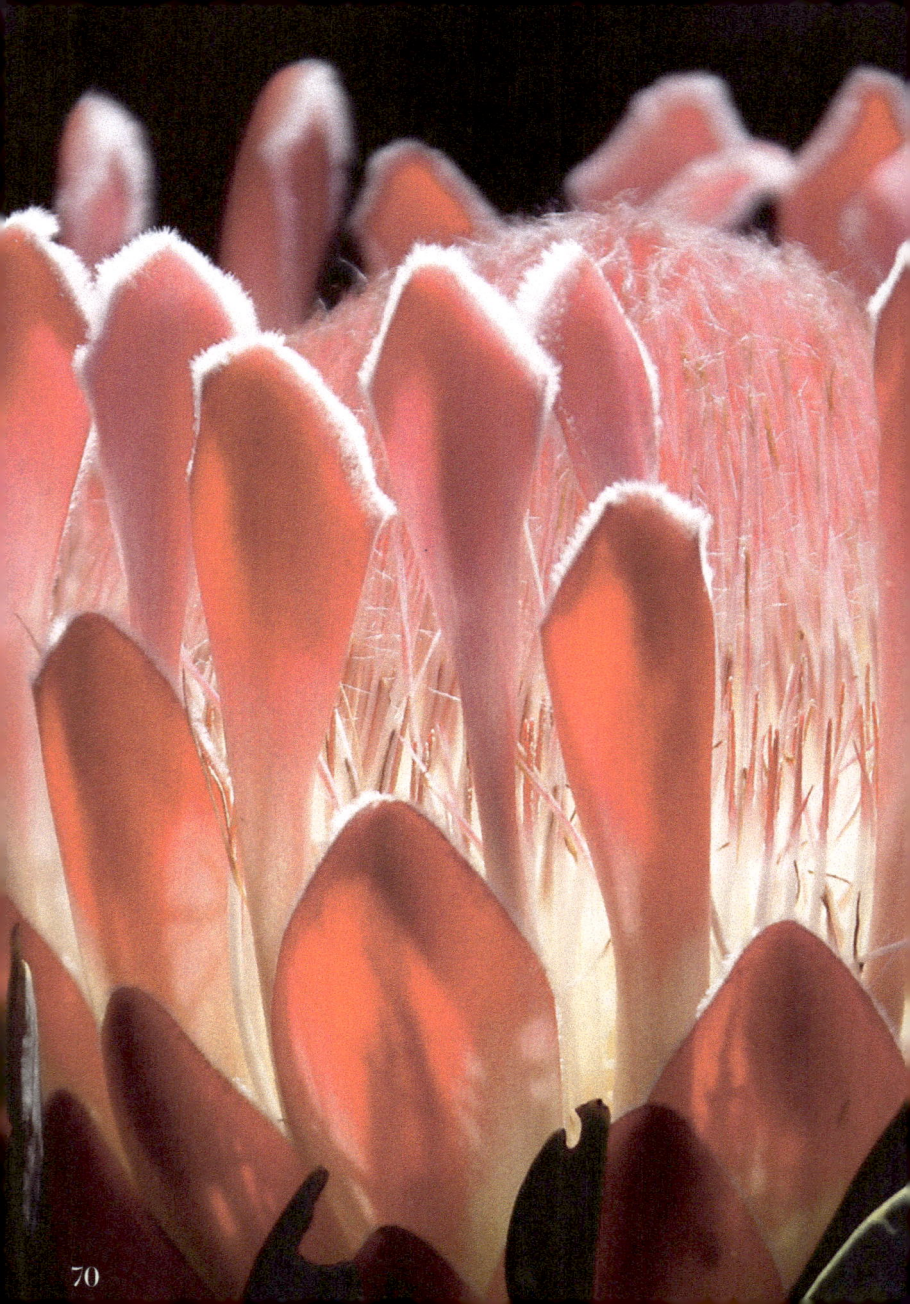

Since love grows within you,
so beauty grows. For love is
the beauty of the soul.

Saint Augustine of Hippo
354–430

Love is composed of a single

soul inhabiting two bodies.

Aristotle
384–322 BC

Love is a smoke raised with the fume of sighs;

Being purged, a fire sparkling in lovers' eyes;

William Shakespeare
1564–1616, Romeo and Juliet

At the touch of love everyone becomes a poet.

Plato
428–348 BCE

Each kiss a heart-quake...

Lord Byron
1788–1824, Don Juan

Love is the master key that opens

the gates of happiness.

Oliver Wendell Holmes
1809–1894

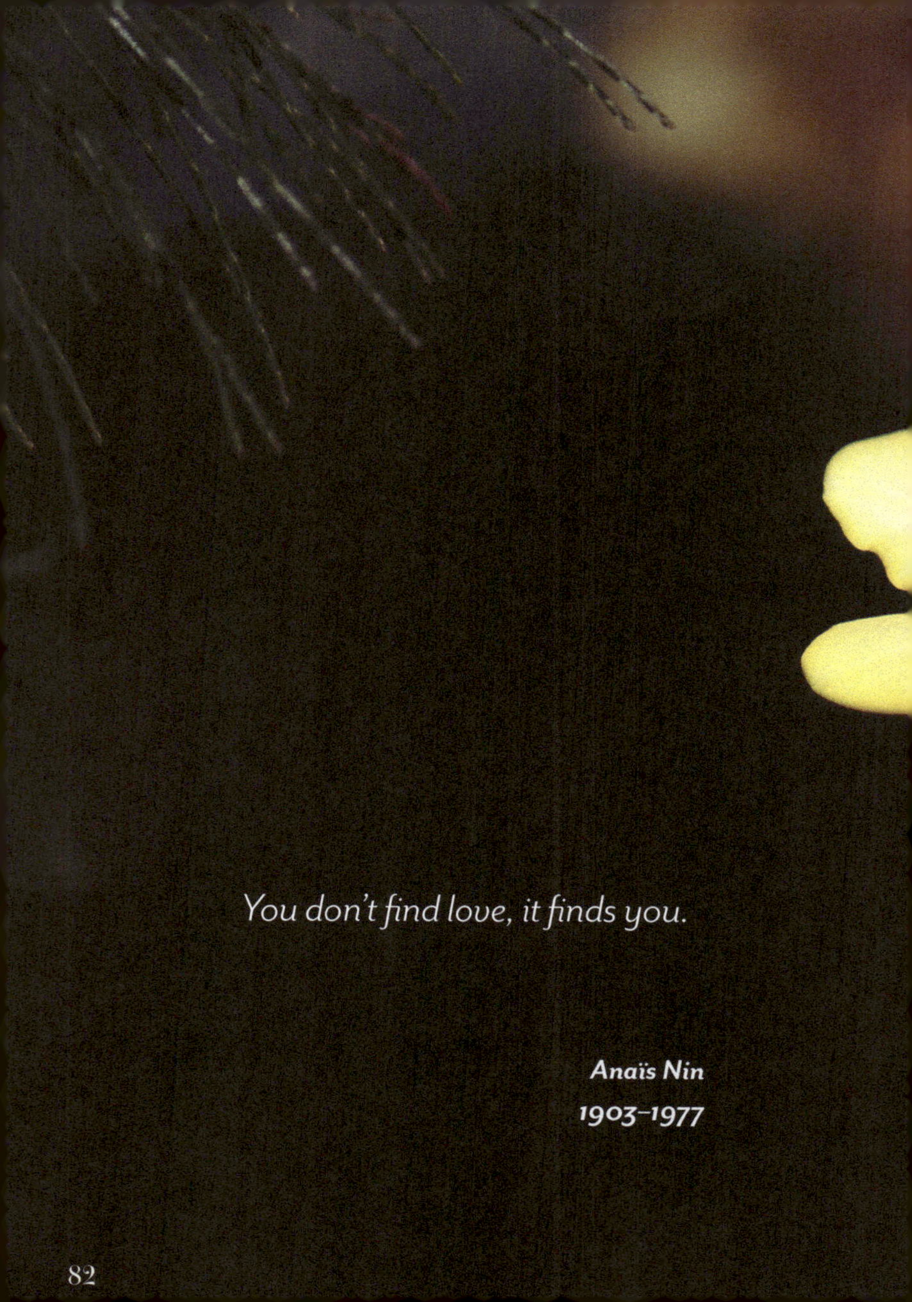

You don't find love, it finds you.

Anaïs Nin
1903–1977

Till I loved I never lived—enough.

Emily Dickenson
1830–1886

Love is life. All, everything that I understand, I only understand because I love.

Leo Tolstoy
1828–1910

Love liberates, it doesn't bind.

Maya Angelou
1928–2014

I love you not because of who you are,

but because of who I am when I am with you.

Elizabeth Barrett Browning
1806–1861

There is only one happiness in life,

to love and be loved.

George Sand
1804–1876

About the Editor

Chrissie Anthony is the romantic alter ego
of Melbourne author, Christine Lister.

How Do I Love Thee? is Chrissie's second book.
Her first book was ***Quiver — Awakening
The Goddess Within***.

For more about Chrissie's books
www.chrissieanthony.com

For more about Christine's books
www.australianinspiration.com.au